Pumpkin Chucking

Pumpkin Chucking

POEMS BY
Stephen Scaer

ABLE MUSE PRESS

Able Muse Press

www.ablemusepress.com

Printed in the United States of America

Library of Congress Control Number: 2012952829

ISBN 978-1-927409-12-1 (paperback)
ISBN 978-1-927409-11-4 (digital)

Cover images: "Accessing Grace" by Abhishek Joshi /
         "Pumpkin Patch" by Dani Foster Herring /
         "Matchstick Trebuchet 3 (Medieval Catapult)" by Eduard Dubrovskis

Cover & book design by Alexander Pepple

Able Muse Press is an imprint of *Able Muse:* A Review of Poetry, Prose & Art—at www.ablemuse.com

Able Muse Press
467 Saratoga Avenue #602
San Jose, CA 95129

For Beth

Acknowledgments

I am grateful to the editors of the following journals where many of these poems originally appeared, sometimes in earlier versions.

The Aurorean: "Eulogy for a Robin."

Bumbershoot: "Mid-Life Limericks."

Classical Outlook: "Twelve Labors."

Cricket: "Left."

First Things: "Backyard Triumph," "Pumpkin Chucking," "The Sacrifice of Cain."

14 by 14: "Say Nothing but Good."

The Formalist: "Hannah at Ten."

Highlights for Children: "Door."

Iambs & Trochees: "The Procession of Elagabalus," "Rental Storage."

Light Quarterly: "Advice to My Tuxedo Cat," "Classical Limericks," "Don Juan of Double-A RP," "Epitaph for Mrs. Lot," "The Frog's Lament," "Gluttony," "Malediction for the Driver on the Cell Phone Who Made Me Miss the Light," "Panegyric," "Pluto's Demotion."

The Lyric: "College Visit," "A Crumpled Leaf," "Gold Is the Last to Leave," "Gray Squirrel Winter," "Leaving Calypso," "Raspberry Patch."

Measure: "Mentor," "Sarcasm," "Sightseers."

The Nashua Telegraph: "To a Pig Dying Young," "Wicked Good Advice."

National Review: "Exposure," "My Familiar Dream."

Not Just Air: "The Beer Commercial."

New England Shakespeare Festival: "For Pity's Sake."

Raintown Review: "Light Box," "To Congress RE: My Legacy."

Texas Poetry Journal: "Hard Times at the Colosseum."

Open any recent American literary journal and you will see the work of the literary heirs of Sylvia Plath, William Carlos Williams, and John Ashbery. Open a British journal and you will see heirs of the same poets along with heirs of Ted Hughes and a few other British poets.

Some of our most remarkable poets have relatively few heirs because their achievement is too distinctive and difficult for most poets to emulate. For instance, one can Google hundreds of uses of the adjective "Larkinesque," but one can search for quite a while before finding a poet other than Philip Larkin himself described in that fashion.

Robert Frost occupies a similar place in our poetic pantheon. Although Frost was the last poet to make a major impact on both American literary and popular cultures, it is difficult to identify many heirs to the Frost legacy other than Timothy Steele, Richard Wakefield and Robert Crawford.

With the publication of Stephen Scaer's *Pumpkin Chucking*, we have a poet who can make a case for being a legitimate heir of Frost. His work celebrates the New England landscape while still being universal, it uses form in an accomplished and inventive fashion, it reserves metaphor and grand statements for the moments that require them, and it surprises us with wit in the winking way of Frost.

The title poem supports these points. Instead of treating a New England ritual as an opportunity for postmodern snark or a launching pad for a self-absorbed lyric, Scaer treats the scene with both humor and respect. He lyrically captures the essence of the participant's motivation, the joy of the "unexpected grace" of a soaring object, and perhaps also their relief in not having met "their sticky end."

Approaching mortality is a key theme of *Pumpkin Chucking*. Scaer approaches our time-limited lot not in a "woe is me" fashion, but in a clear-eyed and poignant way. Scaer's sense of being on the losing end of a generational shift makes "Hannah at Ten" a splendid poem. The reader will appreciate his clear-eyed description of a vibrant daughter, but that appreciation will become even more resonant as the poet becomes "grateful" for the time with her and all too aware of his growing irrelevance to a life that is still arcing upward.

"College Visit," a kind of sequel to "Hannah at Ten," echoes many of the same themes without being repetitive. It begins with an understated quotation that captures both the awkwardness and the strength of this father-daughter relationship as the daughter enters adulthood:

I'm sorry, Dad. You need to wait out here.

Frost himself would have admired that start to "College Visit."

Scaer's sense of mortality even becomes fodder for his self-deprecatory humor. In "Time Management" the poet makes Stephen Spender's mistake of comparing himself with the truly great, and then laconically realizes that he is not even close to their achievement and losing time to catch up:

Today I slept late, took a walk,
sipped coffee on my ragged lawn,
checked the mailbox, saw the clock,
and noticed half my life was gone.

Scaer's humor actually outdoes Frost's and is closer to X.J. Kennedy's; there are many hilarious poems in this collection. Some of the titles will make you hurry for the laughs that will follow, as with the wonderful "To a Pig Dying Young." His "Prayer for a Meeting" finds badly needed humor in the workplace, but it also rises to another level of wit in its conclusion:

> . . . so I'm able
> to be content in everything, like Paul,
> who loved those whom he didn't like at all.

He can even make spousal murder funny with this genially befuddled ending:

> My wife, should I do something to displease her,
> would never stoop to anything that drastic.
> But then, why does she want a bigger freezer?

Finally, again like Frost, Scaer is a master of iambic pentameter who can skillfully use a wide range of meters and forms for his purposes. Perhaps the finest two lyrics in this collection are in shorter meters. The lovely "Gold Is the Last to Leave" is in rhymed iambic trimeter and the gemlike "Crumpled Leaf" is in the even more challenging rhymed iambic dimeter. He also uses an Anglo-Saxon accentual line to set up the masterful mock-heroic tale of "Wendell."

Able Muse Press has done us all a service by giving us this first book of Stephen Scaer.

—A.M. Juster

Contents

Pumpkin Chucking

Hannah at Ten

She hops Monadnock's cliffs, a restless bird,
chattering nonsense to the April dawn,
not caring how the wind distorts each word
since she has words to spare. She prattles on
about the elms that twist to reach the sun
and rest against the ledge on gnarled knees.
They're ogres, she pretends, and talks to one
who claims the mountain witch turned them to trees.
She pauses just a moment from her talk
to follow veins of quartz across a stone.
Her father's grateful he's allowed to walk
beside her, knowing soon he'll walk alone.
In time he'll wonder where the ogres went—
old trees, old men become irrelevant.

Say Nothing but Good

We pulled your funeral off without a hitch.
Morticians had to spread a pound of wax
across your face to smooth away the cracks
that spilled your brains into a roadside ditch.
Your youngest child, the one you nicknamed "Bitch,"
described your death, revising awkward facts.
She said you called before God swung the ax,
"As if to say goodbye." Oh, that was rich!
She didn't mention how you begged for money
to head downtown to finish getting plastered
and rent a prostitute. It's almost funny
how much we love you dead, and quite a show
we've put on in your memory, you bastard.
I wish that we had done this years ago.

Mid-Life Limericks

I've learned to pretend that I am
a graying, compassionate lamb.
It appears that I care,
but in fact when I stare
at you blankly, I don't give a damn.

From my photos I know it appears
I've been losing my hair through the years.
But I'm not—there's no lack
on my belly or back.
I've got hair coming out of my ears.

I don't drink to excess anymore,
and I work at the gym till I'm sore.
I'm trimmer and stronger,
I'll likely live longer,
but would someone remind me what for?

We should lay in provisions for snow
like the pioneers. Darling, we know
that our winter supply
very soon will run dry,
and the knees aren't the first things to go.

Time Management

Luther, in the year he spent
as Junker Joerg in Wartburg towers,
translated the New Testament
to pass away the idle hours.

While living as a refugee,
Erasmus wrote his tour de force:
in *Praise of Folly*'s said to be
the product of a trip by horse.

With dinners late, D'Aguesseau saw
an opportunity to write
his sixteen-volume work of law
in fifteen minutes every night.

Today I slept late, took a walk,
sipped coffee on my ragged lawn,
checked the mailbox, saw the clock,
and noticed half my life was gone.

Pumpkin Chucking

Every Columbus Day
the locals bring their chairs
and watch a trebuchet
launch pumpkins at a fort
of tin, as engineers
at play attempt to crush
the record for the sport
of hurling giant squash.

It must have been a shock
when such a monster threw
silent rounds of rock
into the market square
hundreds of years ago.
But the Big Moons they hurl
today could only scare
the unsuspecting squirrel.

These fruits are much too soft
to crack a citadel.
Some prove, while still aloft,
unequal to the stress
of flight and send a hail
that's tragically organic.
They spread a pureed mess
but hardly cause much panic.

In spite of all the gore,
there's an unexpected grace
in how the pumpkins soar
over treetops and descend
like basketballs from space.
Though like all living things,
they meet a sticky end,
at least, they've had their flings.

Sightseers

The tourists pause for photographs and call
their relatives to brag about the yachts,
the crystal breakers shattering on the wall,
the mansions yearning seaward from their lots.
A few will spend a moment there alone,
transported to a gentle century—
a garden party held on polished stone
where ladies in white dresses serve them tea.
But soon the dream dissolves. They grow aware
of boys performing backflips off the rocks
for college girls who sunbathe almost bare.
They join their friends to shop along the docks,
or head to their hotel rooms, two by two,
since, after all, a view is just a view.

Mentor

Now thirty-some years on, my palms still hurt
when I recall how Miss Sedelski stalked
among the rows of desks, and if I talked,
she called my name in measures soft but curt,
and crossed the room. She wore a miniskirt
and candy-apple boots, and when she walked
she swayed like swing set chains. With her eyes locked
on mine, she meted out my just desert.
Lost in her scent, the sting left by her ruler,
I acted up again. "Let's try your right."
Whack – whack – whack, her blows much crueler.
My mother asked me why my grades turned bad,
as if I knew what kept me up at night
as tortured lyrics filled my spiral pad.

Wendell

Wendell Whitenose   whistle-whirler
broad-chested, brown,   summer blond
feasted on cheesesteaks   furnished by chicklets
who stayed near his stand   to stare at his muscles
their bodies glistening   before him on beach towels.

No vixen could draw   his vision from duty.
Thane of the Poconos   his perch was his throne.
His shades shone,   burnished shields
daring delinquents   to run on the dock
his throat sounded   thunder threats
when scofflaws threw sand   or swam past the buoy line.

Once there was one   who wouldn't obey—
blotched gray and black   red moons on his belly
a wandering water snake   who worried the swimmers
when cottagers crowded   canoe-bearing waters.

Mrs. Weinhoffer wailed   waxen with blood fright
and led a stampede   leaving the lake.
Her hare-hearted husband   held that the snake
was a venomous viper   proved by his pattern.
Mrs. Cummings, the chair   of the Cottagers' Club
demanded the beach   barred to bathers
till someone had slain   the freshwater serpent.

Bold with Ballantine   Ralph Brueninger
wide-bottom warrior   wielding a sand rake
slashed the milfoil   missing his mark
as the hideous head   dodged his hacking.

Despising danger   Wendell descended
and winded his whistle   demanding the waders
stride to the shore.   He strapped on a cooler
emblazoned with Moxie   and made through the muck.
Wendell watched   panther patient
marking movements   the ripples that ran
through its wake as it went   and when it emerged
aching to breathe   the August air
he seized the serpent   holding its head
with thumb and forefinger   through its thrashing
until it tired.   He laid the lake-bane
in the calm-dark cooler   cracking the lid
for the creature to breathe.   He boarded his boat
and soon gained his goal   of the cove by the Girls' Camp
where he let the snake slither   through stump-ragged swamps
no longer a nuisance   to lovers of nature.

The elders applauded   awed by his actions.
But Jenny who sold   soft serve at the Junction
saw Wendell's hand   was harmed in the holding
and balmed the bite wound   with antibiotics.

Wendell aware   his beach days were waning
spoke to the cottagers   in spite of the sting:

"Friends, I must fare   to the hall of my fathers
for August is ending   and I must enter
employment at Allstate   with brothers and uncles
when done at DePauw   this coming commencement,
no more to save   the soused swimmers
or deliver your daughters   with cross-chest carries."
Then Wendell Whitenose   hung his whistle
on Steve, his assistant   who slept in his chair.

The cottagers cried   and prepared a pyre
for pulled pork   at a Labor Day picnic
held in his honor.   That night Wendell heaved
yards of Yuengling   by the yellow-warm fire.
He woke in hell   head hammering
and boarded a bus   to the kingdom of bureaucrats
where monsters are known   by number and name.

Preparing for Flight

The strip mall trapped the wind on Temple Street.
I paused to watched a plastic sack that swirled
with taco wrappers, leaves, the odd receipt,
between Frank's Package Store and Workout World,

and thought of you: when you were only four,
the creatures of backyard imaginings
promised you a graceful set of wings.
Although you don't discuss it anymore

—your classmates taught you not to dream aloud—
I've noticed how you stare into the sky,
longing to disappear behind a cloud
to mountains where your storied kingdoms lie.

That night I dreamed I caught the plastic sack,
and held it out in front and felt it pull
me through the trees, and it seemed plausible
that as my dream dissolved I'd bring it back.

I woke with empty hands. A poor provider,
I tried to think what I could substitute
for wings: a half an hour on a glider,
a bungee jump, a chance to parachute,

but knew that your demands were much too narrow.
I couldn't make you drop your dreams of flight
by tempting you to jump from a great height
and flutter down to earth, a stricken sparrow.

I've often wondered if I wasn't wrong
to read you stories as you went to sleep
that you believed, and stringing you along
with promises no talking fish could keep.

And as we read, I should have let you know
what wasn't real? I left you stranded by
a palace you can never occupy,
and when you turn away, where will you go?

My Familiar Dream

I often have a dream, piercing and strange,
about a girl I love, who loves me too.
Though every night her features might seem new,
her love and understanding never change.

She sees into my heart; its darkness clears.
For her alone, alas, it doesn't pose
a problem anymore. Alone she knows
how to refresh my fevered brow with tears.

Blonde, brunette, or red? I can't be sure.
Her name, as I recall, was sweet and pure,
like those of banished souls whom we once loved.

Her eyes are like a statue's eyes of stone;
her voice is grave, and quiet, and removed,
and has the tone of cherished friends now gone.

Translated from the French of Paul Verlaine

Moonlight

Your soul's a garden in the countryside
where rustic maskers frolic arm-in-arm
or play the lute. Exotic costumes hide,
almost, the sadness in their easy charm.

And though they're singing in a minor key
of how love conquers all, they do not quite
pronounce the words with any certainty,
as their song mingles with the silver light:

the moonlight, heavy with beauty and regrets,
that falls on trees and fills the birds with dreams,
brings sobs of ecstasy from water jets,
the gushing marble fountain's slender streams.

Translated from the French of Paul Verlaine

Resignation

When I was young I dreamt of Persia, Rome,
the Kōh-i Nūr; the opulence and treasure
of emperors who drowned themselves in pleasure.

I staged my plays beneath a golden dome
where I heard music, smelled perfume, and saw
the endless harems of my Shangri-La!

Though I've matured, I'm no less passionate.
Because I've learned what life expects of me,
I've had to curb my lovely reverie,
but haven't yet resigned myself to quit.

I've missed the great, but will not condescend
to settle for polite and commonplace.
I'll always hate a merely pretty face,
a poem that's weakly rhymed, a prudish friend.

Translated from the French of Paul Verlaine

Franconia Notch

You pretend the trees have paved our way
along the stream with bronze; these pillars hold
a limestone sky above a hall of gold—
a game of metaphors we used to play.
My eyes are on the ridge we hiked today,
two four-thousand-footers in the cold.
I feel them in my hips, I'm getting old,
too old to think of anything to say.
You take my hand, trying to make me see
how this late aster really is a star,
how the petals spread like rays. It starts to snow,
and I insist we hurry to the car;
afraid to play, for when my thoughts run free,
they take me places I don't want to go.

You Wear the Heat of Summer

You wear the heat of summer
on your unblemished skin;
the coldest heart of winter
is buried deep within.
But that will change, my darling,
as clocks and seasons spin,
your cheeks will wear the winter,
while summer burns within.

Translated from the German of Heinrich Heine

Crumpled Leaf

A crumpled leaf
scraped down the street
through pewter mist,
and at my feet
it promised me
mortality.
The news it told
was getting old,
since I'd had grief
enough that day.
I turned away
to let it find
an optimist—
a southern mind.

Anniversary InSinkErator

The stream beneath the site of our proposal
at Vista Valley Country Club's faux bridge
has brought us here to shop for a disposal
on Friday night at Lowe's on Sunset Ridge,
uphill from Toys"R"Us. Our love was founded
and sealed when we agreed to wear these bands.
These symbols of infinity surrounded
the two of us in youth. Now we're old hands,
who throughout thirty years have learned to wipe
bottoms and tears, and that these rings of gold
are nothing more than tiny bits of pipe—
expensive plumbing with a bent to hold
resentments since we plug them with our fingers.
Tonight we'll buy a ring where nothing lingers.

Footnote to Psalm 90

So teach us to number our days, that we may apply our
hearts unto wisdom.

May God forbid a CPA, mid-life,
should mull about the things he didn't do,
and buy a bike, a skull-and-bones tattoo.
His calfskin leggings won't impress his wife.
And he can ride his ass to Kathmandu,
Sturgis, South Dakota, or Khartoum,
if he demands a little bit of room.

Lord, why do your lessons come too late,
and by the time I've learned them, don't apply?
For instance, the exchange of eye for eye.
I realize now when I was in grade eight
I should have beat the shit out of the guy
who sucker-punched me. Shown I wasn't weak.
Ignored my pastor's "Turn the other cheek."

The lesson should have been "You won't do time."
It's much too late to fight at 51.
Nor did you say the girls who called me "Hon"
and held my hand when I was in my prime
might dance with nice young men, but had their fun
with idiots before they settled down
with actuaries in a bedroom town.

This is your cruelest education Lord:
you wait until I'm overweight and gray
to teach me to subtract each numbered day,
and then remind me of the flaming sword
you placed to keep me going back that way
to change the stupid things I did before.
It's not my game. Why make me keep the score?

Classical Limericks

As Hector was starting to lag
in the contest of capture-the-flag,
a charioteer
with an oversized spear
convinced him that war was a drag.

Actaeon, the innocent schmuck,
could tell he was plumb out of luck
when he started to stare
at the wrong derriere,
and Diana made change for a buck.

When Daphne provided a moral
example by turning to laurel,
Apollo said, "true,
I've a splinter or two,
but my girlfriend and I never quarrel."

When Dido was burning with shame,
it's said she was heard to exclaim
when she jumped on the pyre:
"Try running, you liar!
You'll never escape your old flame!"

Persephone's mom was astounded
at the way that her girl was impounded.
She announced to King Hades,
"Make sure the young lady's
at home before March or she's grounded!"

Cassandra predicted the course
of the Greeks' disingenuous force.
Though labeled a quack,
she made out at the track.
The lady could sure pick a horse.

The Frog's Lament

The word is out that I'm a prince
trapped in a spell and ever since,
among the royals it's a fad
to stand in line to see my pad.
At first I thought it all a hoot.
(A French girl said my legs were cute).
I'm swamped with debutantes to kiss,
but where's my metamorphosis?
My blood runs cold. What are the odds
that all these princesses are frauds?

Light Box

The customer reviews at Amazon
convinced my wife the UV-filtered rays
emitted by this artificial dawn
would mitigate my seasonal malaise.

But I pretend this light was gathered by
a boy who spooned reflections from the sea
one humid afternoon. Knowing the sky
would dim when autumn came, he thought of me:

staring out the window at the gloom
of snow-banked, yellow streets, and left a box
of summer in a corner of my room
to tide me over till the equinox.

Although his plastic pail might get me by,
I'd love to reach into his summer day
and steal his sun and hang it in my sky
to shine in place of summers thrown away.

Sarcasm

He stuns her with a well-directed word,
measuring her expression as it stings.
Although she acts as if she hadn't heard,
he's in no rush. The epithets he flings
are meant to slowly penetrate her mind,
exposing hidden weakness and self-doubt.
She'll lie awake, aware she's been found out,
as accusations grind, grind, grind.

He cuts her to a manageable size,
and for a moment feels he's in control.
When need arises, he'll apologize,
but what's been torn is never really whole.
The saccharine words and gestures will not close
the wounds he found so easy to expose.

Rental Storage

Detectives couldn't help but like her style.
She shot him twice and kept him mummified
in rental storage, telling friends he died
by accident. She never went to trial.
Although by most accounts the smell was vile,
no tell-tale heart accused her when she lied.
She kept her conscience free of homicide
by trusting in the power of denial.

So when I pass a corrugated shed,
I picture husbands stored in Ziplock plastic
for thoughtless words or words they left unsaid.
My wife, should I do something to displease her,
would never stoop to anything that drastic.
But then, why does she want a bigger freezer?

Prayer for a Meeting

Come, Holy Spirit, fill me with affection
for sycophantic colleagues who pretend a
boss's remark is witty; the projection
of PowerPoints that stray from the agenda
with pie charts, false and darkly personal,
that narrow my dominion to a sliver,
and bullets saying things are worse in all
of my performance measurements. Deliver
your lamb to valleys where he'll safely graze,
or help me love your children at this table,
to hold my tongue, unless to sing your praise
in every situation, so I'm able
to be content in everything, like Paul,
who loved those whom he didn't like at all.

Backyard Triumph

Truant from April chores,
I daydream in a chair
beneath a tree that scatters
its petals when it stirs
the way a girl might scatter
blossoms before a litter
that brings a self-made god
exultant down her road,
while Calvinistic bees
insist that glory's brief.

Extend the allegory:
should petals fall before me?
I've not been made aware
of having won a war,
and I did not design
a bridge or new vaccine.
The leaves against my fence
betray my indolence.

This fragrant celebration
might be for anyone.
I know it's undeserved
but that has not deterred
me from taking pleasure
in the soft spring weather.
The triumphs that I seek

are held for their own sake,
and shower us with grace
like petals on the grass.

Raspberry Patch

Grown-over and grasping   east of my garden,
its barbed branches   bar my passage.
Shoots languish   lost in leaves
clogging the ground   with clumps of decay.
I'll prime this patch   by pulling the puncture weed,
the whips that wrap   around my wrists,
marking my skin   with scarlet stripes.
I'll dig out the dead   canes from the dirt,
biblical chaff   to burn in a barrel.
Red canes will curve   burdened with clusters
of sweet berries   summer-soft and smacking
of exile and effortless   harvests of Eden.
In the cool of the day   I'll come to this corner,
bundled in bathrobe   to bring you fruit
in brimming bowls   to share at breakfast.

Leaving Calypso

Tired of wandering the island's shores
gathering splintered timber at low tide,
I begged my mistress for a list of chores—
some carpentry to keep me occupied.

The sea nymph's grotto had no crooked door
or leaky cedar roof I could repair.
She needed me for love, nothing more.
And love it was—convinced of my despair,

she freed me, though she couldn't understand
why I'd be fool enough to risk my life
to slumber in a bed I made by hand,
or trade a goddess for an aging wife.

College Visit

"I'm sorry, Dad. You need to wait out here."
The tour group rounds the corner out of sight
to visit rooms where they might sleep next year.
A sign proclaims NO MEN. I hope it's right.

Before we leave, she asks to walk alone
to see the grounds and buildings of the school
missed by the tour. I wait for her to phone,
by Churchill's statue in the vestibule.

I take a wingback chair and eat my lean
pastrami (half the sodium and fat)
and watch the passersby—modest, clean.
Some stop to introduce themselves and chat.

I spent those years resisting growing up,
insulting business majors on the quad.
It's too late for me now. I've drained my cup,
and several more, but how I wish to God

that he'd revealed to me the things that they know,
these students who rehearse their final form:
adulthood comes the way a calm volcano
lulls a town before a firestorm

erupts and smothers us in ash, encloses
our attitudes like victims in Pompeii.
I hear a distant rumble as she poses
with Churchill, and I hurry her away.

For Pity's Sake

You say you only come here out of pity,
as if you think there's something wrong with that.
Now, if you loved me just because I'm pretty,
you'd only stay until I'm old and fat.
Love built on common interests would survive
till one of us found better things to do.
Infatuation's only known to thrive
in gardens that it's unaccustomed to.
Romantic love eventually deserts you
when candlelight begins to be a bore,
but charity's the beatific virtue
that comforts the oppressed and feeds the poor.
So if it's what it takes to make you stay,
I plan to grow more pitiful each day.

Exposure

The wind is much too strong. He stoops for shelter
where a split rock hides a narrow patch of grass
beneath the summit shining like stained glass,
and sees the sun go down on his adventure.

He thinks about the shell he didn't pack.
He has a box of matches, but no fuel,
and when the weather changed he was a fool
to push on when the ranger said go back.

He knows it's cold. When he exhales, the steam
solidifies his beard against his face.
But he is summer warm and folds his fleece
on a smooth stone and curls into a dream:

six angels from the AMC hut climb
the ridge to feed him coffee and massage
his limbs before they bear him to their lodge.
He watches as their ponytails keep time.

If only he looked eastward he would find
a cabin waiting with a stove and bed
by Lonesome Lake two hundred yards ahead.
Exhausted hikers rarely face the wind.

Gluttony

We started out with Nachos drowned in cheese
and chili from a can—the family size,
sauce hot enough to make the devil wheeze,
and burgers with hydrogenated fries.
The fudge parfaits that blotted out the skies
with clouds of mousse took all our fortitude.
In our descent we felt our courage rise,
since nothing whets an appetite like food.

Dick Cheney slides his Whoppers down with ease,
and doesn't stew about his swollen thighs,
while Clinton likes to pack his arteries
with Happy Meals and crispy apple pies.
Let surgeons fix each vein that calcifies!
But all this talk just puts me in the mood
to sample something bigger than my eyes,
for nothing whets an appetite like food.

Why should I live in fear of heart disease,
trade living well for eating what is wise?
To starve on skinless chicken breast and peas
would be a life of timid compromise.
Give me the breaded pork that satisfies.
Don't tell me that it's wrong to run on crude.
You've heard my stomach rumble its replies,
since nothing whets an appetite like food.

The King of Burgers never vainly sighs.
So what if he's repulsive in the nude?
Within his chambers true contentment lies,
and nothing whets an appetite like food.

Panegyric

An oyster oozes calcium
to hide its irritation.
Likewise, you have often been
a source of inspiration.

Epitaph for Mrs. Lot

She was driven to distraction.
Now she helps with winter traction.

Eulogy for a Robin

Sweet heralds of the spring,
there's one less singer with us.
My cat seems far too satisfied,
this pile of feathers—suspicious.

To a Pig Dying Young

The time we hauled your derriere
in triumph from the county fair,
the townsmen hailed you as a fine
example of a Yorkshire swine.

Today, the cheering sounds are still,
but for the sizzle of my grill,
as once again we hoist your weight,
but on a bun or paper plate.

You showed good taste, pig, to surrender
your meat while it was moist and tender.
It's better you don't live to see
another pig claim victory.

Eyes I've filled with apple smoke
won't notice there's a hog who broke
his record for the plumpest lard
wallowing in the neighbors' yard.

Still carrying the 4-H prize
for your delicious shape and size,
you've trotted off and won't endure
obscurity—you've found a cure.

Escorted by the King of Beers,
you leave this marinade of tears,
with which all mortal flesh is basted,
and rest assured yours won't be wasted.

Don Juan of Double-A RP

The decades haven't left me weak.
The ladies on the beach agree
my weathered Florida physique
is godlike, dripping from the sea.
I'm out at sunrise for tai chi.
I'm lithe and lean and broad of shoulder,
and measure every calorie,
but still I can't help growing older.

My internist knows each technique
to keep me clog and polyp free.
Things looked up when they took a peek
inside—my colonoscopy,
surveyed my gizzards in 3-D.
He placed a picture in a folder,
a plump manila potpourri
that documents my growing older.

If you want love, my darling, speak;
but please be patient, *ma chérie.*
Though I'm an operable antique
I've outlived any warranty.
We'll spend the evening pleasantly—
if I can't burst in flame, I'll smolder.
Don Juan of double-A RP,
but even I am getting older.

No lady in the home would be
unsatisfied to have me hold her,
so sit on my prosthetic knee,
and please forgive my getting older.

Beer Commercial

When I was only seventeen I thought
romance was like a TV ad for beer.
A cheerleader, her blouse tied in a knot
that bared her abdomen, would come and pour
a glass for me. At once we reappear
among smart friends in some exotic spot
for volleyball and lobsters on the shore,
then spend the evening smooching on a yacht.
Since then I've come to terms with love's demands—
a long commute down 93 at dawn,
then home to screeching brats with sticky hands.
But Sundays when the Patriots are on,
I dream of you with pom-poms, doing splits,
while pouring me a frosty glass of Schlitz.

Malediction for the Driver on the Cell Phone
Who Made Me Miss the Light

When you've finished shopping, may there be
a single line staffed by a young trainee,
with twelve old ladies, chirping, "Just a sec!"
while fumbling for a coupon and a check.
May you discover after having stood
an hour that your credit isn't good.

Unlikely Pair

*NH Historical Society's bobblehead series includes Chief
Passaconaway, a leader of the Pennacook tribe, and
Hannah Duston, who killed and scalped her Native
American captors during a daring escape.*

Wickety, Whackity,
Chief Passaconaway's
bobblehead honors his
peaceable pacts.

Undiplomatically,
Duston is grinning and
wearing a nightgown while
wielding an axe.

To Congress, RE: My Legacy

When you create my federal holiday,
as someday you inevitably will,
don't make it like the one for MLK
and give Americans more time to kill
in front of their TVs or on the slopes.
I wouldn't want our children getting dumber
with me as their excuse. Instead, the dopes
should have an extra day of school mid-summer.
Let teachers (without pay of course) provide
a frankly accurate curriculum.
Don't cover up my faults. Why should I hide
the vices that I've tried to overcome?
You won't improve their morals if you teach
ideals that only Galahad could reach.

Their parents shouldn't be allowed to swill
Corona Light with lime or congregate
with flabby relatives around the grill.
Encourage them to do the things they hate
and haven't gotten to. It's time to scour
refrigerators, seal the asphalt drives,
and Red Sox fans should spend at least an hour
discussing carpet swatches with their wives.
Old England had a day in late December
when children who committed no offense
were soundly beaten so that they'd remember
King Herod's slaughter of the innocents.
I trust that you can find a similar way
to make an impact on my holiday.

Can Someone Do the Math?

Hey, Johnny, you can use a calculator
so you won't hold up our curriculum.
You may not know what's lesser than or greater,
or tell apart a difference from a sum,
but we're past making change. Proponents
of higher learning (Berkeley PhDs)
say to practice negative exponents,
to operate among parentheses.
Don't worry, kid—though you can't play a scale,
it's time to try Rachmaninoff's sonata.
Just do your best, and should your efforts fail
to please the audience, at least we've taught a
creative song with higher-level skills,
and education's more than boring drills.

Opposites

Down

The opposite of down is down.
Were you to tunnel from your town
until you popped out of a hole
in Shanghai, Tokyo, or Seoul,
you'd notice, after close inspection,
that though you keep the same direction,
you switch—by going down you rise.
Forgive me if I emphasize
my logic's sound. You must admit
that down and down are opposite,
unless of course the term referred
to fluffy feathers from a bird.
Its opposite I've not been told.
I'm certain it would leave me cold.

Door

What is the opposite of door?
A gap that lets the north wind pour
a blast of icy arctic air
into the comfort of your lair.
This opposite is far from pleasing
to someone who's opposed to freezing
and likes to read beside the fire
wearing comfortable attire.
I like a solid door that locks

and opens to a friend who knocks.
If cats could talk, then mine would say
that I should take my doors away,
or try to keep them open wide.
They always want the other side.

Left

The opposite of left is right,
which seems a prejudicial slight
to those of us who use our left.
It's also sad that one who's deft
is dexterous, and we infer
that lefties must be sinister
and gauche. It's time that we demanded
that adjectives be even-handed.

Ottoman

The opposite of ottoman
is felt by little children when
you offer them too high a chair,
and let their feet hang in the air.
It hurts to leave one's legs aloft,
so prop them up with something soft.

But if I lived near Istanbul,
I'd need to make it capital:
if it's of kingdoms that I speak,
the local opposite is Greek.

Pluto's Demotion

What gives some supercilious group
the gravitas to tell
this chilly little underdog
that he can go to hell?

And why should common labels change
to taxonomic wishes,
so dolphins and beluga whales
aren't classified as fishes?

But my koala's still a bear,
and I don't think it's cute
to drop a planet from the sky
or call tomatoes fruit.

My Ptolemaic universe
allows me still to know
a sweet potato as a yam,
bison as buffalo.

Like Adam I will name the things
that God designed for me.
To abrogate this sacred task
to nerds is blasphemy.

Wicked Good Advice

For Tying Your Nuptials

Does she love you for you or your stock?
Test her faith with a counterfeit rock:
should she have it inspected,
and your suit is rejected,
then at least she'll have nothing to hock.

For Shoveling Snow

If you're weary of shoveling, I
would suggest that you give this a try:
send your grandma to stand
with a shovel in hand
till a soft-hearted neighbor comes by.

The Procession of Elagabalus

The senators beheld his frilly tunic,
his golden gown, and hair arranged with ribbon,
his entourage: a harem and a eunuch
(see Vol. I, *Decline and Fall* by Gibbon).
His entrance seemed, to Romans crowded near it,
to usher in an age beset with scandals.
This hedonist who lacked a martial spirit
would leave his realm susceptible to Vandals.

My dear, I'm like that city by the Tiber.
Your touch leaves me too indolent to fight,
unraveling each thread of moral fiber,
indulging my licentious appetite.
I open up my gates to my decline,
and swallow you like undiluted wine.

Hard Times at the Colosseum

This season's bread-and-circus programs bore us.
Our rulers hold the door for each invader,
risking our city's fall, but will not cater
to virile Roman tastes. They used to lure us
with naval wars, but now the floor's gone porous.
Last year we watched a girl—I used to date her—
play with a lion, and I was glad he ate her.
Today we're treated to an all-castrato chorus,
sponsored by the Council for the Arts,
proclaiming that poor Alaric's our friend,
and we should leave the Visigoths alone.
We Plebeians want blood, not bleeding hearts.
What's worse, the guards have yet to apprehend
the Christians who've been hauling off our stone.

Twelve Labors

I

Our hero was told to begin
with a lion. He wrestled to win
the over-stuffed hide,
but his stole terrified
Eurystheus out of his skin.

II

On his second Hellenic campaign
a serpent with more than one brain
succumbed to his whacks.
Through his searing attacks,
he diminished its capital gains.

III

For over a year he was stuck
in the woods, but he didn't have luck
in completing his task
till he happened to ask
whether he could just borrow a buck.

IV

It's alleged he committed a break-in;
grew mad after having partaken
of the Centaurs' red wine,
and behaved like a swine
before coming home with the bacon.

V

He cleaned out in less than a day,
three decades of gormandized hay,
for he could deliver
the force of a river
or two—there was no EPA.

VI

He was given some clappers to play
to the birds, and he drove them away.
Their revenge was deferred,
but they have the last word—
they still shit on his statues today.

VII

Eurystheus sent him to Crete
with instructions that he should defeat
a fierce head of cattle
in hand-to-hoof battle.
Then the king turned it loose on the street.

VIII

The most challenging story, of course, is
the tale of the flesh-eating horses,
since the climax and ending
differ greatly depending
on what your original source is.

IX
The Amazon tribe was averse
to his gender—it could have been worse.
Though it made his blood curdle
to shop for a girdle,
no one asked, "Would you please hold my purse?"

X
Though the bulk of the legends are thrillers,
his roundup is one of the fillers:
his head proved to be
much better than three.
On the way, he erected two pillars.

XI
It's strange that he wasn't suspicious
when a Titan he met became vicious,
and taught him to bear
the world and its care,
then brought him the Golden Delicious.

XII
In the last stage, our hero was bound
to the emperor under the ground.
When he asked for his pet,
the planetoid let
him ascend with the three-headed hound.

Gnomology

In the garden behind my grandmother's home,
beneath the tall ferns, is a slumbering gnome
who isn't disturbed in the least that he's sleeping
in the path of a diligent gnome who is sweeping
with a broom made of twigs, while another small man
is making the rounds with a watering can.
He's learned that it's better to lie in the shade
than push a wheelbarrow or dig with a spade,
for whether gnomes labor or hide from the sun,
none of them really gets anything done.

Darkling Bat

Squatting upright on my kitchen floor,
an embryonic terrier taken wing,
squawked a warning, daring me to bring
around my broom and swat him out the door.
Throwing a slow curve to dodge my swing,

it fluttered twice around my head and darted
into the yard, where I could barely see
a nodule bulging from a hemlock tree
behind the house, twelve yards from where it started.
I watched it, grateful for the company

of someone else who hoped the day would end.
That morning, I believed the thrush's song,
but his bright day turned cold and overlong.
My small black dog, my pessimistic friend,
would never let me down if he proved wrong.

Gray Squirrel Winter

His kingdom isn't of the earth,
but in red-oak branches where he's built a berth
from scraps of cardboard, leaves and plastic straws,
and lined the walls with glossy Sunday fliers,
to take a hypothermic pause
from dodging dogs and tires.

But from his louse-infested bed,
this stylite, cloaked with hair, who begs for bread,
stirs in his winter-torpor dreams and sees
dominions branching out from his abode:
cross-continental canopies
unbroken by a road.

The Swift

That trickle in the storm drain was the Swift,
a river where nomadic hunters drank
from waters wide and deep enough to lift
a narrow ship. The wells along that bank,

by Wimpy's parking lot, were once so pure
the pilgrims thought their source must be divine.
There's Mary's Inn where gentry took the cure;
behind the iron fence, a limestone shrine.

In time the city dammed the stream for mills,
clogged it with dead horses, rotting malt,
and from its birthplace in the northern hills,
they buried it inside a chambered vault.

But for the stench, you wouldn't know it's there—
inside its narrow dungeon where it waits
for a March storm to stir it from its lair,
and send it burbling through iron grates,

flooding basements, leaving wallboards rotten,
and joining tributary streams to claim
the valley that it's never quite forgotten,
and course along the street that bears its name.

Up Late

For A.S.

My scheming nine-year-old won't put away
his scattered picture books, his nests of clothes,
and Lego fortresses because he knows
his weary mom will find them when the day
is through. He waits upstairs for her to say,
"Come back and put away your things!" He throws
the covers back and, right beneath her nose,
he heads into to the living room to play.

I plan to do the same when my day ends.
When just before my bedtime God assesses
my legacy—neglected bills and friends—
he'll be disgusted, give me extra time
so I can organize my lifelong messes.
I'll squander it on daydreams, books, and rhyme.

4 a.m. Argument with Larkin

When your head aches from your fifth glass of scotch
and keeps you up, your oak wardrobe assumes
a threatening identity. You watch
it until dawn, pretending that it looms
closer every night—a bogeyman.
Though no one else has seen the beast, you can.
So tangible is your oblivion,
you smell the mold and incense on his breath.
Each night you meet with death,
who makes all thoughts impossible but one.

It isn't really that you fear the void,
for who has never longed to disappear
into the perfect sleep described by Freud?
How else could you be anywhere but here,
inside a person you don't like too well.
And though you claim to see, through Heaven, Hell,
the truth is you don't want a home on high.
You're looking for a kinder God who'll give
another chance to live
the life you had, the life you let pass by.

And it's not really death who stalks you, is it?
It's the fat-cheeked little girl you never kissed,
the son in Manchester who doesn't visit,
the freckled grandson: none of them exist.
This prison barge can only move one way,

and you're chained to the oarlock of today.
It's obvious why thoughts of death attract you
when you have neither company nor drink,
nothing but time to think—
your churning mind needs something to distract you.

The yellow morning edges through the curtain.
Behind it lies a village, clean and stark
as hospital walls. You wish you weren't so certain
that it's still there: the snow-encrusted park,
the station where the 8:16 will carry
you to your desk, your loaf-haired secretary.
You have to rise, exchange an empty bed
for work, while jukeboxes of might-have-been
continuously spin
78s that never leave your head.

The Sacrifice of Cain

Even as a child, I understood
why God refused to try his sacrifice,
but he considered Abel's offering good.
The Lord of Hosts is not above a slice
of marinated lamb on applewood.
Cain offered what?—burnt watercress and rice?
I would have sent that vegetarian
to wander through Nod's deserts there and then.

Like Adam's sons I offer up my gift—
a rack of ribs I'm smoking with mesquite.
Not *soli Deo gloria*—I lift
the incense of my herb-encrusted meat
for all humanity. With every shift
of wind, it enters houses on my street,
accompanied by bottleneck guitar,
and spiced by my Dominican cigar.

But as with any blessing of the spirit,
I'm not surprised to see my gift rejected
by stony-hearted Pharisees who fear it
could cause them cancer, and the disaffected,
music-hating neighbors who have no ear, it
would seem, for blues, and will not be subjected
to a fat man who lets his lawn revert
to jungles where he walks without a shirt.

I wish I were a better man. My face
is marked for mediocrity. The year
meanders past, not pausing to replace
neglected lovers, mend a blown career.
But there are compensations for disgrace—
this lilac-shaded hammock, horseshoes, beer.
And I'm in no position to decline
whenever God provides an anodyne.

Gold Is the Last to Leave

The sugar maples hold
the budding April gold
of florid carotene
masked within the green
of summer's chlorophyll,
until the frosts distill
the yellow in the leaf.
So age refines the grief
that never found reprieve.
Gold is the last to leave.

Long Trail

You can spot the better hikers by
the lightness of their steps, and how their packs
seem much too small. They've learned they shouldn't try
to carry their whole lives across their backs.
Inside their tidy rectangles they keep
the minimum they need to make their homes.
They eat two protein bars and fall asleep,
snug inside their instant nylon domes.
Though I go hiking several times a year,
I always carry much more than I need:
outside, my pack is hung with cooking gear,
inside, the books I probably won't read;
and when I raise my tent, unwelcome guests
crowd a cluttered mind that never rests.

Photo by Bethany Poulin

Stephen Scaer of Nashua, NH, is a special education teacher with poems published in *National Review, First Things, Cricket,* and *Highlights for Children.*

ALSO FROM ABLE MUSE PRESS

www.ablemusepress.com

www.ingramcontent.com/pod-product-compliance
Lightning Source LLC
Chambersburg PA
CBHW021426090426
42742CB00009B/1269